A CAITLYN DLOUHY BOOK

ATHENEUM BOOKS FOR YOUNG READERS
New York London Toronto Sydney New Delhi

To all the librarians—
the tellers of tales
—ADW

To those
who dare to jump and
those who give us a place
to land
—JA

jump
at
the
sun

The True Life Tale
of Unstoppable Storycatcher
Zora Neale Hurston

Alicia D. Williams

Illustrated by Jacqueline Alcántara

IN A TOWN CALLED EATONVILLE—
a place where magnolias smelled even prettier
than they looked, oranges were as sweet as they
were plump, and the people just plain ol'
got along—lived a girl who was attracted
to tales like mosquitoes to skin.

Zora was her name.

Zora got to lovin' tales from hearing the townsfolk swap stories at Joe Clarke's general store. Oftentimes Mama sent her over to fetch a li'l sugar or salt, and Zora would stall, make a ten-minute errand last an hour, just to overhear tales like how that trickster Brer Rabbit always got the best of Brer Fox. Only thing pulled her away was Mama calling:

"Zora-a-a! If you don't come here, you better!"

When there were no errands to run, and Zora couldn't get
an earful of tales, she'd make up her own. She'd fashion dolls
from scraps she found. A loose doorknob became Reverend Door-Knob;
the do-not-touch Pears' scented soap was carved into Mr. Sweet Smell;
ears of corn were hewed into Miss Corn-Shuck and Miss Corn-Cob.
Zora had stories to tell, and stories needed characters!

And when Mama sent Zora and her stories out of the house, Zora'd perch herself atop their gatepost, calling out to travelers: "Don't you want me to go a piece of the way with you?" If a car stopped, Zora climbed right in. She'd have those people laughing like she was storytelling on Joe Clarke's porch herself, then, half a mile or so later, she'd hop out and stroll on home.

Now, back then, some folks called storytelling "tellin' lies," and if Zora's preaching papa got home from church and caught her spoutin' 'em, he'd give chase lightning-quick. Even Zora's grandma aimed to sting her backside, but never could, not with Mama's arms stretched wide as tree limbs. Truth was, Mama approved of Zora's storytelling. She didn't fancy the idea of her children tilling land, so she encouraged Zora to "jump at de sun. You might not land on de sun, but at least you'd get off de ground."

Well, fact is, Zora clung to those words tighter than Brer Fox would've clung to Brer Rabbit, if he'd ever been able to catch him. Zora needed 'em, too, 'cause one day, Mama got herself a chest cold that wouldn't get better.

Then one September evening, Mama closed her eyes for the last time. Zora and her sister and brothers were so sobbing-hearted that even the house seemed to mourn.

Two days later, Zora's only sister and an older brother headed back to school. Papa was already on the road preaching. His boys seemed manageable, but his tale-telling girl was too much for him to worry about. So, two weeks after the funeral, he shipped Zora off to Florida Baptist Academy boarding school.

Zora dug her nose in books, intent on reaching the sun. It was what Mama had always taught her to do, after all. Then her papa got a new wife who was stingier than a peacock! Zora's stepmother tightfisted their money, school fees went unpaid, and back to Eatonville Zora went.

To hear Zora tell it, back home, "The walls were gummy with gloom" with her little brothers in "ragged, dirty clothes." This was wrong, and Zora made it known. Fussin' and fightin' commenced from the kitchen to the gatepost.

Finally, her stepmother pointed to the door, and out stomped fourteen-year-old Zora down the dusty road.

Though friends spared a pallet for sleeping, there wasn't time for Zora to be pondering the capers of Brer Rabbit.

She had to earn her keep. But she was better at storytelling than holding a job. She was fired from maid jobs (for reading the employers' books, steada cleaning).

She up and quit babysitting her oldest brother's children (when he quit on his promise to let her go back to school). For twelve long years, she traveled from job to job, from Florida to Baltimore, in and out of schools.

Zora was miserable—except for when she spooned out Eatonville trickster tales to whoever'd sop 'em up. And, sakes alive, folks were hungry!

The sun, however, was getting antsy waiting on Zora, so he called down, saying, "Ain't you s'posed to be meeting me up here?" Reckon Zora was getting antsy too.

How was Zora to jump all the way to Ole Big Yellow? By doing what made her happiest. And Zora was happiest at school and hearing those stories.

In Baltimore, twenty-six-year-olds couldn't go to public school for free. So Zora told a tale of her own: she chopped her age to sixteen, then plunked herself down in a high school classroom. Even though she had a lot less money than the other students, Zora walked through the halls like her shoes were lined with gold. That girl was back in school, whooey!

The sun waited patiently for two more years, until she graduated, then called out, "Jump, Zora."

· So she did, to Howard University! The best part? All those years of tarrying around Joe Clarke's and making up tales out of corn husks paid off. She shared her tales with the director of the Stylus, the college's literary club, and was offered membership. Zora not only wrote for their magazine, but the door opened to other events where she met successful writers like W. E. B. Du Bois, who wrote a book she loved, *The Souls of Black Folk*. Soon she got to thinking: *I want to be a famous author too.*

So Zora jumped again. She got herself a typewriter, and her fingers got tah tappin' and all her Eatonville memories poured into them pages. One of her stories was even about a little girl, sitting atop a gatepost!

Though Zora loved her schooling, she found she loved writing more. And at that time, new writers who wanted to get published went to one place. So, in January 1925, Zora made her way to New York City. As in Eatonville, folks welcomed her.

During the day, she listened to book discussions at the library or lectures at the YMCA.

Come nighttime, Zora'd be
swinging in Harlem, where Count
Basie or Fats Waller pounded on
the piano, and folks danced
the Charleston.

Once her feet were too sore for one more kick, Zora would hold court, surrounded by writers like Arna Bontemps, Fannie Hurst, and her best pal, Langston Hughes. Langston's poetry jumped at the sun, for sure! If Zora's stories held the ears of these great writers, surely her mama was right that Zora could really reach the sun too.

That spring, Zora jumped again.
She mailed a handful of stories to
a magazine's literary contest. Her
words were so alive that the judges saw
the moss on the trees, smelled the
saw grass in the Everglades, and heard
the men chanting on the railroad. Then
those judges began chanting Zora's name:

HONORABLE MENTION, SHORT STORY . . . "Black Death" by Zora Neale Hurston!
HONORABLE MENTION, PLAY . . . Spears by Zora Neale Hurston!
SECOND-PLACE FICTION AWARD . . . "Spunk" by Zora Neale Hurston!
SECOND-PLACE DRAMA AWARD . . . Color Struck by Zora Neale Hurston!

A fancy college heard about Zora's storytelling and offered her admission. But if there was one thing Zora had learned, it was that school was expensive, and she didn't have two nickels to rub together. Zora was doubtful. **"Jump, Zora,"** Mama's words sang.

And wouldn't you know it, her jumping paid off. Barnard College offered her a scholarship! It wasn't much, but friends helped out.

And Zora put together a collection of tales from home, called it "The Eatonville Anthology," and earned a bit from that. For the first time in all her schooling, Zora was able to **stay** in school.

For her very last semester, Zora had one big project left to do: fieldwork for her anthropology class. Anthropology is the study of humans and their behavior. Her professor, Dr. Boas, suggested that Zora collect Negro folklore.

Now, folklore includes stories and beliefs passed down from generation to generation, 'zactly like the ones told at Joe Clarke's. Shucks, Dr. Boas might as well have asked Zora to go down to Joe Clarke's for some sugar!

And that Brer Fox threw Brer Rabbit right into the thicket!

There once was this fella named John Henry. Now, he wasn't no ordinary man, you see.

Just 'cuz he drank up his water?

She had heard Brer Rabbit's adventures, and why the squinch owl screeched, since she was a baby.

How many lumps of sugar had she fetched to hear about High John de Conqueror!

Or how many times had her mama called "Zora-a-a"?

Course she'd go collect some stories!

What's a squinch owl?

Now, it's a loud screeching owl that once was a . . .

Zora looked up to the sky: *I'm coming for you, sun.*

And the sun smiled down: *I know.*

Zora drove into Eatonville, and even after she'd been gone for twenty-two years, the townsfolk still recognized her.

"Well, if it ain't Zora Hurston!"

They rattled off questions before she could even answer 'em.

"You gointer stay awhile?"

Several months . . .

"Where you gointer stay?"

I reckon . . .

"What you up to?"

Ah come to . . .

Zora, at last, sat on Joe Clarke's store porch. The townsfolk ate gingerbread, drank buttermilk, and commenced to woofing about John and de frog, the man who went to heaven, and Jack and the Devil. As the menfolk plucked their guitar strings, it's said that even the moon dipped lower to get an earful of tales.

But outside of Eatonville, folks zipped their lips to the meddling stranger with the notebook and northern accent. To ease their minds, Zora spun a believable tale about her own self: "I'm a bootlegger, running from the law." The folks then trusted she wasn't just snooping and offered her a treasure of folklore.

Went down to the river Heard a mighty racket Nothing but de bull frog Pullin' off his jacket!
It was a man, and he was so big and fat till he went to whip his little boy for something. The little boy run up under his papa's belly and hid up under there for six months.
Ah'm tellin' dis lie on de 'gator. Well, de 'gator was a pretty white varmint wid coal black eyes. . . . So one day he was layin' up on de grass in a marsh sunnin' hisself and sleepin' when Brer Rabbit come bustin' cross de marsh and run right over Brer 'Gator . . .

Zora's college project became one of her biggest jumps.

Even after she graduated, she didn't
stop collecting tales.

She trekked all the way from Alabama to New Orleans to Haiti
and the Bahamas, gathering as much folklore as a leopard has spots.

And then she *stopped* jumping,
long enough to take her notebooks
and tapes and find herself a home in
Eau Gallie, Florida.

There, on her porch, with papers spread out, Zora took her biggest jump ever. She set up her typewriter, and her fingers got tah tappin' all those tales into books. Then she tapped up her very own stories and made her own books, too.

Zora—like her mama always dreamed—reached the sun.

And now, when you open those books, it's as if you were visiting
on Zora's porch just like she porch-visited all those years ago; she'd've
offered you a chair and filled you full of High John de Conqueror tales.
Or told you the talking mule lie she got from the Florida railroad workers.
Course she'd woof about that ol' Brer Rabbit and Brer Fox, too.

And that sun ... that sun would've beamed down
mightily pleased, just ah-listening.

Author's Note

I remember when I first met Zora. I was in college, studying in the library. My friend, only a table over, giggled and giggled. She'd get quiet and then giggle again. Finally, I got up from my seat to find out what was so funny. She held up a book by Zora Neale Hurston. And she later gifted me the anthology *I Love Myself When I Am Laughing . . . And Then Again When I Am Looking Mean and Impressive.* This book is in my collection to this very day.

Zora Neal (without the *E*) was born in Notasulga, Alabama, on January 7, 1891 to sharecropping parents John Hurston and Lucy Potts Hurston. In 1892 the family moved to newly established Eatonville, Florida, and from there, Zora's life became a journey of adventures.

It was deeply inspiring to learn of this unstoppable storycatcher who'd hopped into her Ford coupe, aptly named Sassy Susie, and traveled throughout the South's back roads during a time of lynching and Jim Crow laws. Zora similarly traversed the deepest parts of Haiti, Jamaica, and the Bahamas and amassed cultural songs, dances, tales, religious practices, and children's games, so that we all may enjoy them today. If it is true that we learn from our ancestors, then her folklore collection is a vast treasure of knowledge.

Novelist, folklorist, and anthropologist were not Zora's only roles. During the Great Depression, President Franklin D. Roosevelt initiated the Works Progress Administration, a program that employed millions of jobseekers and artists. In 1935, Zora was a dramatic coach for the Federal Theatre Project, and in 1939, she worked for the Federal Writers' Project. She was awarded a Guggenheim fellowship to study in the West Indies. Zora also established a dramatic arts program for educator and civil rights activist Mary McLeod Bethune's college, Bethune-Cookman College, and taught drama at North Carolina College for Negroes, which is now named North Carolina Central University. And in 1939, Morgan State College awarded Zora with an honorary Doctor of Letters.

Zora garnered numerous awards for her plays, articles, musical revues, and novels, yet she never received the financial gains that she deserved. In her later years, she worked as a librarian, substitute teacher, and even a maid to survive. After suffering a stroke in 1959, she was forced to move into St. Lucie County Welfare Home. On January 28, 1960, Zora died from hypertensive heart disease and was buried in an unmarked grave. In 1973, beloved author Alice Walker located Zora's grave and honored her with a tombstone with the inscription "'A Genius of the South' . . . Novelist, Folklorist Anthropologist."

Sixty years later, Zora's writings are still being published. In 2018, *Barracoon: The Story of the Last "Black Cargo,"* comprising her 1927 interviews with Cudjo Lewis, the last survivor of the last known American slave ship, was finally published.

Zora Neale Hurston is indeed a national treasure.

I hope you, dear reader, will fall in love with Zora and her tales, just as I have.

I would like to thank Dr. Karla Holloway, professor, author, and Zora Neale Hurston scholar, for generously reading my manuscript.